INSPIRATIONAL HOLLYWOOD:

Reflections on Life, Love, and the Art of Filmmaking

selected and compiled by

Ronald Warren Deutsch

Published by Michael Wiese Productions, 11288 Ventura Blvd., Suite 821, Studio City, CA
91604   (818) 379-8799   Fax (818) 986-3408.
E-mail: wiese@earthlink.net
http://www.mwp.com

Cover Design by Art Hotel, Los Angeles
Book Layout by Gina Mansfield Design
Final Copy Check by Bernice Balfour

Printed by Braun-Brumfield, Inc., Ann Arbor, Michigan
Manufactured in the United States of America

Library of Congress Cataloging in Publication Data

Inspirational Hollywood : reflections on life, love and the art of filmmaking / selected and
compiled by Ronald Warren Deutsch.
        p.   cm.
    ISBN: 0-941188-63-9
    1. Motion picture actors and actresses -- Quotations. 2. Television actors
    and actresses -- Quotations.
I. Deutsch, Ronald Warren. 1955 -
PN1994.9.I48   1997
791.43--dc21   97-26510
                                                                        CIP

To Francis X. Feighan who in both life and death, inspired me to make this happen and see it through.

I would like to thank a number of people who helped with the creation of this book -- my publisher Michael Wiese, his staff, and in particular Ken Lee; my legal beagle Louise Nemschoff; all my friends who took the time to pick the choice cuts, especially Jennifer Heftler and Lisa Page-Kissig, Tony Colitti, Max Kovins, Christine Trepczyk, and the Weeks family; Franklin C. Baer of Baertracks for help with sourcing; and everyone else I've ever met who've both encouraged or discouraged me because they only make me stronger.

And so I don't get any flack about leaving her out -- my Mom.

When first approached to put together this collection, there were two thoughts that ran through my mind. One was that it would be quite easy. The second, that I was at a point in my life in which I was nearly totally fed up with the machinations of Hollywood and was perhaps too cynical to write something inspirational about it. Nevertheless, I took on the task.

To my first thought, I quickly discovered that if you were to write a book about people bad-mouthing this business, you could probably do it in a day. While one can sit in coffeehouses and bars in Los Angeles and listen to those who haven't made it complain about the unfairness, the toughness, and the stupidity that sometimes seems to rule over this town, it seems those who are succeeding don't often find satisfaction once they get there. I was finding stacks of quotes by actors, writers, and directors with nothing nice to say. This fed my second thought — it doesn't matter if you're successful or not, you have to be a masochist of the highest order to try and pursue a showbiz career. How was I going to write this book?

As I immersed myself in looking for quotes, pulling books I hadn't peeked through for years off dusty shelves, something happened. Here was a quote that made me smile, one that made me laugh, and another that made me think. I'd find passages and quotes I'd underlined when I was still a bright-eyed and bushy-tailed kid hoping someday to show the world what I could do. And I couldn't shrug these feelings away. The words of these artists started to do their magic on me. And by the time I finished pasting all the quotes into my computer and seeing them there all together, the spell was cast. In the same way after going to see a great film, watching a brilliant performance, listening to dialogue that ripples and tickles the soul, I was renewed. And if the words collected in this book had that effect on a world-weary person like me, I feel sure they can work on you.

While many of these quotes deal with the art of filmmaking, others remind us there is more to life than work and that our work depends on our life. For it is our lives and the lives of others that inspire us. Without life, love, death and taxes, what would writers write about? Directors direct about? Where would be the emotions actors must tap into to create their memorable characters? Perhaps in no other business or craft do the things that lives are made of become so inseparable and sometimes so confused between the light and the shadow. These quotes offer both advice and solace from fellow dwellers in this strange world.

So let me thank all the artists whose quotes are collected here for inspiring me, and I look forward to hearing how they have done so for you. If only one quote in this book makes you have the strength to go to yet another casting call, start or finish that screenplay you've been avoiding, pick up that camera and make the movie you've dreamed of, or find that passion or muse that so often escapes us in both life and work, then its purpose is served. And if you get the part, sell the script, win the Oscar and get quoted in the paper, remember to give something back. Find a few words to inspire those waiting in the wings. Besides, I'll have more material then for the second edition.

Ronald Warren Deutsch
May 17, 1997

*I love quotations because it is a joy to find thoughts one might have,
beautifully expressed with much authority by someone recognized
wiser than oneself.*

— Marlene Dietrich

Laughter is an instant vacation.
— Milton Berle

Humor is just another defense against the universe.
— Mel Brooks

You grow up the day you have the first real laugh — at yourself.
— Ethel Barrymore

I had stumbled upon the secret of being funny: an idea going on in one direction meets an opposite idea suddenly.
— Charles Chaplin

Laughter is much more important than applause. Applause is almost like a duty. Laughter is a reward. Laughter means they trust and like you.
— Carol Channing

Foolishness is infinitely more fascinating than intelligence, infinitely more profound. Intelligence has limits while foolishness has none.
— Claude Chabrol

He who laughs most, learns best.
— John Cleese

One doesn't have a sense of humor. It has you.
— Larry Gelbart

*The oddest thing about this whole funny business is that the public
really wants to laugh, but it's the hardest thing to make them do it.
They don't want to cry, yet they will cry at the slightest provocation.*
— Harry Langdon

There are three things that are real to me — God, human folly,
and laughter. Since the first two are beyond our comprehension,
we must do what we can with the third.
— Jerry Lewis

The only way to get a serious message across is through comedy.
— Woody Harrelson

The funniest joke of all is the absolute truth stated simply
and gracefully.
— Carl Reiner

Comedy has to be truth. You take the truth and put a little curlicue at the end.
— Sid Caesar

A comedian is not a man who says funny things. A comedian is one who says things funny.
— Ed Wynn

A clown is like aspirin, only he works twice as fast.
— Groucho Marx

*The whole object of comedy is to be yourself and the closer
you get to that, the funnier you will be.*
— Jerry Seinfeld

I'm not funny. What I am is brave.
— Lucille Ball

*Life can be wildly tragic at times, and I've had my share.
But whatever happens to you, you have to keep a slightly comic
attitude. In the final analysis, you have got not to forget to laugh.*
— Katharine Hepburn

If you can't laugh, you're dead. I'm laughing
all the time — you just never catch it.
— Robert Mitchum

In the end, everything is a gag.
— Charles Chaplin

Being a sex symbol has to do with an attitude, not looks. Most men think it's looks, most women know otherwise.
— Kathleen Turner

It's my cameraman who is getting older.
— Doris Day

People go, "Doesn't it bother you when they say hunk?" and you say, "You know what? They're not saying schmuck."
— George Clooney

The way I look at it, I'm a human being first and gorgeous second.
— Harvey Fierstein

Beauty comes in all sizes — not just size 5.
— Roseanne

If you're buying into that perfect body image thing, then you're helping the enemy.
— Janeane Garofalo

I think your whole life shows in your face and
you should be proud of that.
— Lauren Bacall

Nothing in the world can be compared to the human face.
It is a land one can never tire of exploring.
— Carl Dreyer

Sex appeal is 50 percent what you've got and
50 percent what people think you've got.
— Sophia Loren

It is better to be looked over than overlooked.
— Mae West

It's necessary, at some point, to destroy your beauty.
— Raquel Welch

If you haven't cried, your eyes can't be beautiful.
— Sophia Loren

My advice to actresses is don't worry about your looks.
The very thing that makes you unhappy in your appearance
may be the one thing to make you a star.
— Estelle Winwood

If you're born an overstatement and the world sees you as one,
you might as well play it that way.
— Tammy Grimes

I think on-stage nudity is disgusting, shameful, and damaging to all things American. But if I were twenty-two with a great body, it would be artistic, tasteful, patriotic, and a progressive religious experience.
— Shelley Winters

Sex appeal is in your head and heart. I'll be sexy no matter how old or how my body changes.
— Sonia Braga

It matters more what's in a woman's face than what's on it.
— Claudette Colbert

I think the most important thing a woman can have — next to talent, of course — is her hairdresser.
— Joan Crawford

I don't mind living in a man's world as long as I can be a woman in it.
— Marilyn Monroe

There's a little bit of hooker in every woman.
A little bit of hooker and a little bit of God.
— Sarah Miles

God made men stronger but not necessarily more intelligent.
He gave women intuition and femininity. And, used properly, that
combination easily jumbles the brain of any man I've ever met.
— Farrah Fawcett

I'm furious about the Women's Liberationists.
They keep getting up on soapboxes and proclaiming that
women are brighter than men. That's true,
but it should be kept very quiet or it ruins the whole racket.
— Anita Loos

It's possible that blondes also prefer gentlemen.
— Mamie Van Doren

Most women set out to try to change a man, and when they have changed him they do not like him.
— Marlene Dietrich

The average man is more interested in a woman who is interested in him than he is in a woman with beautiful legs.
— Marlene Dietrich

A man is as old as the woman he feels.
— Groucho Marx

If you want to know a man you can find out an awful lot by looking at who he married.
— Kirk Douglas

Men read science fiction to build the future. Women don't need to read it. They are the future.
— Ray Bradbury

A kiss is a lovely trick designed by nature to stop speech
when words become superfluous.
— Ingrid Bergman

Chains do not hold a marriage together. It is threads,
hundreds of tiny threads which sew people together through the years.
— Simone Signoret

The story of love is not important — what is important
is that one is capable of love. It is perhaps
the only glimpse we are permitted of eternity.
— Helen Hayes

Sexiness wears thin after a while and beauty fades, but to be married to a man who makes you laugh every day, ah, now that's a real treat!
— Joanne Woodward

I think all relationships have a sense of comedy to them.
— Deborah Amelon

Love is an act of endless forgiveness, a tender look which becomes a habit.
— Peter Ustinov

How does it happen that something that makes so much sense in the moonlight doesn't make any sense at all in the sunlight?
— Lana Turner

Nudity is easier if there are two of you.
— Greta Scacchi

When two people love each other, they don't look at each other,
they look in the same direction.
— Ginger Rogers

Age does not protect you from love. But love, to some extent,
protects you from age.
— Jeanne Moreau

You can't help getting older but you don't have to get old.
— George Burns

Age is something that doesn't matter, unless you are a cheese.
— Billie Burke

Old age is like everything else. To make a success of it,
you've got to start young.
— Fred Astaire

The secret of staying young is to live honestly, eat slowly,
and lie about your age.
— Lucille Ball

The hardest years in life are those between ten and seventy.
— Helen Hayes

Being angry at twenty is sexy, being angry at fifty is pathetic.
— John Waters

After forty, we are responsible for our own faces.
— Jean Cocteau

It is sad to grow old but nice to ripen.
— Brigitte Bardot

Old age is no place for sissies.
— Bette Davis

The only thing I regret about my past is the length of it. If I had to live my life again, I'd make the same mistakes, only sooner.
— Tallulah Bankhead

Old age isn't so bad when you consider the alternative.
— Maurice Chevalier

The older I get, the more I believe in what I can't explain or understand, even more than the things that are explainable and understandable.
— Lillian Gish

As long as you are curious, you defeat age.
— Burt Lancaster

There is a fountain of youth: it is your mind, your talents,
the creativity you bring to your life and the lives
of the people you love. When you learn to tap this source,
you will have truly defeated age.
— Sophia Loren

A man is not old until regrets take the place of dreams.
— John Barrymore

Too many people grow up. That's the real trouble with the world,
too many people grow up. They forget.
They don't remember what it's like to be twelve years old.
They patronize, they treat children as inferiors. Well I won't do that.
— Walt Disney

Looking at yourself in a mirror isn't exactly a study of life.
— Lauren Bacall

Don't take life too seriously. You'll never get out alive.
— Bugs Bunny

Let the world know you as you are, not as you think you should be,
because sooner or later, if you are posing,
you will forget the pose, and then where are you?
— Fanny Brice

Slow down and enjoy life. It's not only the scenery you miss by going too fast — you also miss the sense of where you are going and why.
— Eddie Cantor

But Jesus, you can't start worrying about what's going to happen. You get spastic enough worrying about what's happening now.
— Lauren Bacall

Life is very simple. The first thing to remember about life is — don't worry about it.
— Milton Berle

*I have no regrets. I wouldn't have lived my life the way I did
if I was going to worry about what people were going to say.*
— Ingrid Bergman

*Living at risk is jumping off the cliff and building your wings
on the way down.*
— Ray Bradbury

*I can't see what's coming, and I like that a lot. It's like standing
at a roulette wheel in Vegas, and your life is the ball.*
— Eric Bogosian

I prefer to be like a gambler: if you don't throw, you'll never know.
— Robert De Niro

I read Shakespeare and the Bible, and I can shoot dice.
That's what I call a liberal education.
— Tallulah Bankhead

See into life — don't just look at it.
— Anne Baxter

If a man does not know what is impossible, he will do it.
— Mike Todd

*I never learned as much in the classroom as I did staring out
a window and imagining things.*
— Robert Redford

Nothing is impossible. Some things are just less likely than others.
— Jonathan Winters

Trust your instincts. If you have no instincts, trust your impulses.
— Noel Coward

The past is a ghost, the future a dream, and all we ever have is now.
— Bill Cosby

I'm for anything that gets you through the night, be it prayer,
tranquilizers or a bottle of Jack Daniels.
— Frank Sinatra

The only thing that matters is experience.
— Michelangelo Antonioni

The more opinions you have, the less you see.
— Wim Wenders

Bad taste is simply saying the truth before it should be said.
— Mel Brooks

I think knowing what you cannot do is more important
than knowing what you can do. In fact, that's good taste.
— Lucille Ball

If you obey all the rules you miss all the fun.
— Katharine Hepburn

The problem with people who have no vices is that generally you can
be pretty sure they're going to have some pretty annoying virtues.
— Elizabeth Taylor

Whenever I'm caught between two evils, I take the one I never tried.
— Mae West

It takes a long time to learn simplicity.
— Louis Malle

Happiness sneaks in through a door you didn't know you left open.
— John Barrymore

We've no control over our conception, only over our creation.
— Tony Curtis

If we could only find the courage to leave our destiny to chance, to
accept the fundamental mystery of our lives, then we might be closer
to the sort of happiness that comes with innocence.
— Luis Buñuel

There's only one thing worse than a man who doesn't have
strong likes and dislikes and that's a man who has strong likes and
dislikes without the courage to voice them.
— Tony Randall

Courage is knowing that there's something to be afraid of
and continuing anyway.
— Meg Ryan

Fear makes you run one way — courage makes you run the other.
— John Huston

Life is hard, and to survive in simple ways is a heroic thing.
— Cameron Crowe

Most of us have compromised with life. Those who fight for what they want will always thrill us.
— Vivian Leigh

Tomorrow is the most important thing in life. Comes into us at midnight very clean. It's perfect when it arrives and puts itself in our hands. It hopes we learned something from yesterday.
— John Wayne

You gotta have a strong sense of self, and your mother's telephone number, so she can keep you in check.
— Wesley Snipes

Be like a duck, my mother used to tell me. Remain calm on the surface and paddle like hell underneath.
— Michael Caine

Never do anything you wouldn't want to be be caught dead doing.
— John Carradine

There is no end. There is no beginning. There is only the infinite passion of life.
— Federico Fellini

I believe in using words, not fists.... I believe in honesty. I believe in a good time. I believe in good food. I believe in sex.
— Susan Sarandon

What you get is a living. What you give is a life.
— D.W. Griffith

Humility and questioning go hand in hand. Humility isn't something you make up. It's... coming up against the great unknown and admitting you just don't know.
— Sam Shepard

You are not punished for your anger; you're punished by your anger....
There's not some moment when you're going to be called to task
because you've been angry, but your anger itself is what punishes you,
limits your life, and constricts you.
— Meg Ryan

Every wonderful thing we want to do in our lives is already in us.
We just gotta find it.
There's nothing we're ever going to do that we can't do right now.
— Jon Turteltaub

Either you decide to stay in the shallow end of the pool
or you go out in the ocean.
— Christopher Reeve

The secret of a happy life is accept change gracefully.
— Jimmy Stewart

A word to the wise ain't necessary — it's the stupid ones who need the advice.
— Bill Cosby

When you learn not to want things so badly, life comes to you.
— Jessica Lange

Nothing trains you for life.
— Mike Nichols

The things we do are never more than the shadows of our dreams.
— Oskar Werner

It is the friends you can call at 4:00 a.m. that matter.
— Marlene Dietrich

We are well advised to keep on nodding terms with the people we used to be, whether we find them attractive company or not. Otherwise they turn up unannounced and surprise us, come hammering on the mind's door at 4:00 a.m. of a bad night and demand to know who deserted them, who betrayed them, who is going to make amends. We forget all too soon the things we thought we could never forget.
— Joan Didion

It's not hard to make decisions when you know what your values are.
— Roy Disney

My mother wanted us to understand that the tragedies of your life one day have the potential to be comic stories the next.
— Nora Ephron

You begin saving the world by saving one man at a time; all else is grandiose romanticism or politics.
— Charles Bukowski

The more fully I grasp not just how a character behaves, but why he behaves, the more I find that my patience with people and my understanding of them grows. I seldom get mad.
— Jack Lemmon

Hindsight is always twenty-twenty.
— Billy Wilder

What's right is what's left if you do everything else wrong.
— Robin Williams

Listen to everybody. Don't believe anybody.
— Henry Jaglom

No one can be exactly like me. Sometimes even I have trouble doing it.
— Tallulah Bankhead

I am more important than my problems.
— Jose Ferrer

Happiness is good health and a bad memory.
— Ingrid Bergman

Everybody's a mad scientist, and life is their lab.
— David Cronenberg

Once you begin to explain or excuse all events on racial grounds,
you begin to indulge in the perilous mythology of race.
— James Earl Jones

I'm black and I've decided I like my color.
Anyone that doesn't that's their worry.
— Sidney Poitier

The racism, the sexism, I never let it be my problem,
it's their problem. If I see a door comin' my way, I'm knockin' it
down. And if I can't knock down the door, I'm sliding through the
window. I'll never let it stop me from what I wanna do.
— Rosie Perez

I love to work, although sometimes I can spend whole days doing nothing more than picking the lint off the carpet and talking to my mother on the phone.
— Beth Henley

I'm a compulsive worker. What I really like to do best is whatever I'm not doing at the moment.
— Woody Allen

I can always be distracted by love, but eventually I get horny for my creativity.
— Gilda Radner

*Love the craft, the practice of your art — in other words, being
on the plateau — and the peaks will come.*
— Dennis Palumbo

I always did something I would do for nothing.
— David Brown

*No person who is enthusiastic about his work has anything
to fear from life.*
— Samuel Goldwyn

One of the things I learned the hard way was that it doesn't pay to get discouraged. Keeping busy and making optimism a way of life can restore your faith in yourself.
— Lucille Ball

I'm always pursuing the next dream, hunting for the next truth.
— Stanley Kramer

This, I believe, is one recipe for happiness; to work with people you love and who love you. The advantage of being eighty years old is that one has had many people to love.
— Jean Renoir

I remember that someone once said that the whole thing is to keep working, and pretty soon they'll think you're good.
— Jack Nicholson

What does method of working matter as long as the result obtained is both poetic and true.
— Vittorio De Sica

Attempt the impossible in order to improve your work.
— Bette Davis

You know how I'm smart?
I got people around me who know more than I do.
— Louis B. Mayer

Always be smarter than the people who hire you.
— Lena Horne

I don't want yes-men around me. I want everybody to tell me
the truth even if it costs them their jobs.
— Samuel Goldwyn

The important thing isn't how many people come to see your work.
The important thing is having to live with it for the rest of your life.
— Terry Gilliam

I don't know anything about luck. I've never banked on it, and I'm
afraid of people who do. Luck to me is something else: Hard work —
and realizing what is opportunity and what isn't.
— Lucille Ball

If your work isn't exciting, doesn't stir emotions, where's the chal-
lenge? Where's the progress if you always play it safe?
— Michael Douglas

When you're experimenting you have to try so many things
before you choose what you want,
and you may go days getting nothing but exhaustion.
— Fred Astaire

If you're going to take a job to live on, make sure it's a job that is
impossible for you, just really unpleasant. That way, you won't ever
get seduced into thinking, "Gee, I really want to park cars all my
life." That helps keep you on track. If you hate what you're doing
every day, it reminds you of what you want to do.
— Lawrence Kasdan

Eighty percent of success is showing up.
— Woody Allen

*Seventy-five percent of being successful as an actor is
pure luck — the rest is just endurance.*
— Gene Hackman

It takes twenty years to make an overnight success.
— Eddie Cantor

You have to believe in yourself, that's the secret. Even when I was in the orphanage, when I was roaming the street trying to find enough to eat, even then I thought of myself as the greatest actor in the world.
— Charles Chaplin

I've never been poor, only broke. Being poor is a frame of mind. Being broke is only a temporary situation.
— Mike Todd

If Hollywood didn't work out, I was all prepared to be the best secretary in the world.
— Bette Davis

*You have to get lucky at some point, but you can only get lucky
if you are still on the road, and for each of us that road,
that journey is of a different length. The thing is to keep doing
it and doing it, any way you can.*
— Lawrence Kasdan

*I pretended to be somebody I wanted to be until finally I became that
person. Or he became me.*
— Cary Grant

If I don't make it today, I'll come in tomorrow.
— Ruth Gordon

Forget the ego, you'll get there. Be real or get out.
— Bruce Dern

My agent said: "You aren't good enough for movies."
I said: "You're fired."
— Sally Field

The higher up you go, the more mistakes you are allowed.
Right at the top, if you make enough of them, it's considered
to be your style.
— Fred Astaire

(Success is) when you don't know if you're working or playing.
— Warren Beatty

There's no deodorant like success.
— Elizabeth Taylor

If you are in a position to give credit yourself, then you do not need it.
— Irving Thalberg

It's better to be known by six people for something you're proud of than by sixty million for something you're not.
— Albert Brooks

You're not a star until they can spell your name in Karachi.
— Humphrey Bogart

There is a gigantic difference between earning a great deal of money and being rich.
— Marlene Dietrich

When you reach the top, that's when the climb begins.
— Michael Caine

I always wanted to be a movie star.
I thought it meant being famous and having breakfast in bed.
I didn't know you had to be up at 4:00 a.m.
— June Allyson

Success is always somebody else's opinion of you; but it doesn't
amount to a damn compared to your own opinion of yourself....
— Jack Lemmon

Many times I wondered whether my achievement was worth the loneliness I experienced, but now I realize the price was small.
— Gordon Parks

I'll match my flops with anybody's but I wouldn't have missed 'em. Flops are a part of life's menu and I've never been a girl to miss out on any of the courses.
— Rosalind Russell

I'm not afraid to fail, providing I fail honorably.
— David Puttnam

I don't know the key to success, but the key to failure is trying to please everybody.
— Bill Cosby

You can't go around the theaters handing out cards saying, "It isn't my fault." You go on to the next one.
— John Sturges

Failure: Is it a limitation? Bad timing? It's a lot of things. It's something you can't be afraid of, because you'll stop growing. The next step beyond failure could be your biggest success in life.
— Debbie Allen

You can't get spoiled if you do your own ironing.
— Meryl Streep

Success and failure in films are exactly the same.
They're both imposters.
— Paul Newman

People often confuse personality with talent.
— Alan Delon

*Talent is the least important thing a performer needs, but humility
is the one thing he must have.*
— Clark Gable

*Having talent is like having blue eyes. You don't admire a man for
the color of his eyes. I admire a man for what he does with his talent.*
— Anrhony Quinn

A career is born in public — talent in privacy.
— Marilyn Monroe

There's never any talent without a little strain of madness.
— Jean-Louis Trintignant

I'm a whore. I go where I'm kicked. But I'm a very good whore.
— Sam Peckinpah

Mystery is the essential element of every work of art.
I shall never tire of repeating this.
— Luis Buñuel

The right to express ideas, good ideas, bad ideas, wild ideas,
crazy ideas, impossible ideas — this is the most precious right
the individual can have.
— Dalton Trumbo

It's kind of fun to do the impossible.
— Walt Disney

You can't make anything be art — and the minute you try,
it eludes you. And if you behave like an artist, you'll never be one.
— Mary Astor

Don't think. Thinking is the enemy of creativity.
It's self conscious, and anything self conscious is lousy.
You can't try to do things. You simply must do things.
— Ray Bradbury

The more things you have done, the less you have to
depend on your imagination.
— William Bowers

Imagination is the highest kite one can fly.
— Lauren Bacall

All artists have one quality that is priceless — eternal childhood.
— Rod Steiger

You're best when you're not in charge. The ego locks the muse.
— Robin Williams

The more you reason the less you create.
— Raymond Chandler

When you do not know what you are doing and what you are doing is the best — that is inspiration.
— Robert Bresson

The artist is simply the medium between his fantasies and the rest of the world.
— Federico Fellini

I just put my feet in the air and move them around.
— Fred Astaire

If you believe in an idea, you don't own it. It owns you.
— Raymond Chandler

A hunch is creativity trying to tell you something.
— Frank Capra

I don't want life to imitate art. I want life to be art.
— Carrie Fisher

Make visible what, without you, might perhaps never have been seen.
— Robert Bresson

I passionately hate the idea of being "with it." I think an artist is always out of step with his time. He has to be.
— Orson Welles

I like pushing the form, over-reaching, going a little too far, just on the edge, sometimes getting your fingers burned. It's good to do that.
— Gay Talese

So what if my telephone is turned off again at home? Or my electricity is shut off? Or my credit cards canceled? If you don't bet, you don't have a chance to win. It's so silly in life not to pursue the highest possible thing you can imagine, even if you run the risk of losing it all, because if you don't pursue it you've lost it anyway. You can't be an artist and be safe.
— Francis Ford Coppola

I don't think it's very useful to open wide the door for young artists; the ones who break down the door are much more interesting.
— Paul Schrader

Despite the culture, an artist must live without fear of emotion, of other types of consciousness, of suprarational experiences.... Let others live in black and white; you must live in Technicolor. And without a subjunctive tense you must still make your reader see the blood at the heart of the ruby.
— Rita Mae Brown

The essential is sufficient.
— Carl Dreyer

Art? You just do it.
— Martin Ritt

A film lives, becomes alive, because of its shadows, its spaces.
— Michael Cimino

A film is the world in an hour and a half.
— Jean-Luc Godard

Each film is a little lifetime.
— John Huston

Film is a battleground: love, hate, action, death. In a word: emotion.
— Sam Fuller

The length of a film should be directly related to the endurance of the human bladder.
— Alfred Hitchcock

I don't try to guess what a million people will like. It's hard enough to know what I like.
— John Huston

Cinema should make you forget you are sitting in a theater.
— Roman Polanski

Hollywood has always been a cage... a cage to catch our dreams.
— John Huston

The cinema has no boundary; it is a ribbon of dreams.
— Orson Welles

The movies are just some shadows that dance on a screen and hold millions of people enthralled.
— Mervyn Leroy

Ours is a business both strange and unique, a business of starlight and glamour — one moment a place of dreams, the next of nightmares.
— Christopher Lee

It's show business. You've got to do a little show and a little business.
— Patrick Duncan

Film is too vast a medium for self-indulgence. It's a dangerous tool and you must be responsible when you use it.
— Fritz Lang

We are in the business to provide entertainment, but in doing so we do not dodge the issue if we can also provide enlightenment.
— Darryl F. Zanuck

Making films solely for entertainment is like making a soup with only one ingredient.
— David Puttnam

For me, the cinema is not a slice of life, but a piece of cake.
— Alfred Hitchcock

Some critics say that audiences complain about the movies because the
movies do not reflect reality; it is this writer's suspicion that
more people lament the fact that reality does not reflect the movies.
—· Leo Rosten

Film is a personal effort and if you fail, you should fail for the right
reasons — it's the only way of growing.
— Dustin Hoffman

It's just as hard to make a bad movie as it is to make a good movie.
— Robert De Niro

No story ever looks as bad as the story you've just bought; no story ever looks as good as the story the other fellow just bought.
— Irving Thalberg

If it's a good movie, the sound could go off and the audience would still have a perfectly clear idea of what was going on.
— Alfred Hitchcock

I say an audience doesn't know what they want to see,
but they know what they don't want to see.
— William Castle

A film is never really good unless the camera is an eye in
the head of a poet.
— Orson Welles

Good films can be made only by a crew of dedicated maniacs.
— Sir David Lean

If there's a way of saying "I love you" without saying it —
that's film.
— Buster Keaton

The actors were all in their places — looking at me expectantly. I'd no idea what was required. Finally, my assistant whispered: "Say action." I did so and The Maltese Falcon was underway.
— John Huston

A director is a ringmaster, a psychiatrist, and a referee.
— Robert Aldrich

The best directors are artists with a touch of showbiz hack in them. Me? I'm a showbiz hack with a touch of artist in me.
— Bob Fosse

For me, directing films is like having sex; when it's good,
it's very good; but when it's bad, it's still good!
— Stanley Donen

To shoot a film is to organize an entire universe.
— Ingmar Bergman

Filmmaking is a cheap way to have therapy.
— Billy Bob Thornton

You can only make the film you're compelled to make.
That's your only responsibility.
— Mary Harron

My commitment is to each story, not to a career.
— Jane Campion

If it can be written, or thought, it can be filmed.
Stanley Kubrick

Give me any two pages of the Bible and I'll give you a picture.
— Cecil B. De Mille

You can make a thousand movies out of one incident.
— Martin Scorsese

I just try to catch the thoughts....
— David Lynch

The task I'm trying to achieve above all is to make you see.
— D.W. Griffith

I leave myself out of my films, and yet I'm in every frame.
— Ken Burns

It's true, I splatter bits of myself all over the screen.
— Martin Scorsese

There are a thousand ways to point a camera, but really only one.
— Ernst Lubitsch

I direct as little as possible. I relieve myself of the ardors of direction simply by casting it right.
— John Huston

I never listen. I watch. And if I believe it, I print it.
— Martin Ritt

*I always think of the audience when I'm directing — because
I am the audience.*
— Steven Spielberg

*I've made mistakes in drama. I thought drama was when actors
cried. But drama is when the audience cries.*
— Frank Capra

The nature of the work is to prepare for a good accident.
— Sidney Lumet

We can't deal with opinions. All we can do is weave a little romance
as pleasantly as we know how.
— D.W. Griffith

I make a film like I cook for friends. I hope they like it, but if they
don't, I'm prepared to enjoy it all by myself.
— Melvin Van Peebles

I wanted to make a film which would be entertaining enough to eat.
— Akira Kurosawa

I have ten commandments. The first nine are thou shalt not bore.
The tenth is, thou shalt have the right of final cut.
— Billy Wilder

We all steal but if we're smart we steal from great directors.
Then, we can call it influence.
— Krzysztof Kieslowski

*If you write a hundred short stories and they're all bad, that doesn't
mean you've failed. You fail only when you stop writing.*
— Ray Bradbury

The difference between fiction and reality? Fiction has to make sense.
— Tom Clancy

*Writing is almost as lonely a craft as flagpole sitting....You write
behind a closed door, and fun is your enemy.*
— Ben Hecht

When you start a movie script, it's like entering a dark room: You may find your way around all right, but you also may fall over a piece of furniture and break your neck. Some of us can see a little better than others in the dark, but there is no guaranteeing audience reaction.
— Billy Wilder

Writers wail about the loss of control when a director goes to work, but I wonder if this loss is actually part of a silent bargain.... Directing entails social and political skills many of us became writers expressly to avoid ever having to develop.
— Joseph Dougherty

Each writer is born with a repertory company in his head.... As you get older, you become more skillful at casting them.
— Gore Vidal

You can't make conclusions about what the script is about until you know what the truth is.
— Jane Anderson

It's only words...unless they're true.
— David Mamet

I ask myself, "What Is forbidden? What can't I write about?" And then I write about it.
— Stephen King

The hard thing about screenwriting is that you have to remain open enough to really feel things, but closed enough not to get killed when stuff goes wrong.
— Audrey Wells

Writing has laws of perspective, of light and shade, just as painting does, or music. If you are born knowing them, fine. If not, learn them. Then rearrange the rules to suit yourself.
— Truman Capote

It is the writer's privilege to help man endure by lifting his heart.
— William Faulkner

Cats gotta scratch. Dogs gotta bite. I gotta write.
— James Ellroy

People want to know why I do this, why I write such gross stuff.
I like to tell them that I have the heart of a small boy —
and I keep it in a jar on my desk.
— Stephen King

Somerset Maugham said there were three rules to writing — and
nobody knows what they are.
— Joan Collins

A good story cannot be devised; it has to be distilled.
— Raymond Chandler

The only time in my life when I've cleaned the oven is when I'm writing. My house is never cleaner than when I'm writing.
— Chris Noonan

Listening is essential in writing and it takes a lot of practice. It's not just listening with the ear, but it's that inner sort of listening. It's like listening to yourself think when you're driving long distances through the night, or listening to yourself play an instrument.
— Sam Shepard

*The drama doesn't lie in the events. It lies in the behavior
of the characters.*
— Martin Brest

*Everybody's on their way to somewhere and very few
people ever get there because too many things happen.
Now, that's simply good dramatics.*
— William Bowers

*It's hard enough to write a good drama, it's much harder
to write a good comedy, and it's hardest of all to write a drama
with comedy. Which is what life is.*
— Jack Lemmon

Drama is life with the dull bits cut out.
— Alfred Hitchcock

That's something you've got to learn about screenwriting — how to fight for what's written but to know enough about movies to know that things do change.
— Mark Peploe

We should never expect that word for word our movies will make it to the screen, because they won't.... {But} if, when they walk out of the theater, they understand what was in your heart when you originally wrote the script, then you've succeeded.
— Jane Anderson

You get a real sense of what the audience recognizes as common to them as a group, the things in you that you thought that nobody else knew about, that everybody else knew about, and you realize it when they suddenly roar with laughter at something you thought no one else had ever felt. And it's the clear laughter of recognition.
— John Patrick Shanley

There comes a point — especially with a joke or a funny scene — where you've read it so many times, everybody is so tired of hearing it, you know the punch line, and it's not funny anymore. You have to remember way back, months before, the first time you thought of it, it was funny, and have faith with it.
— Frank Pierson

If I have anything to say to young writers, it's stop thinking of writing as art. Think of it as work....It's hard physical work. You keep saying, "No, that's wrong, I can do it better." You have an original, fresh concept; you want to fulfill it as precisely and as completely as you can, and in the effort to achieve that, the constant self-demand is, in essence, what art is.
— Paddy Chayevsky

*It took me fifteen years to discover I had no talent for writing, but I
couldn't give it up because by that time I was too famous.*
— Robert Benchley

Let's have some new clichés.
— Samuel Goldwyn

The real actor — like an artist — has a direct line to the collective heart.
— Bette Davis

{As an actor} you're giving people little tiny pieces
of time they never forget.
— Jimmy Stewart

The thing about performance, even if it's only an illusion, is that
it is a celebration of the fact that we do contain within ourselves
infinite possibilities.
— Daniel Day-Lewis

*If you can reveal to an audience what lies within them, you can be
as important as a philosopher, a psychiatrist, a doctor, a minister or
whatever. You have to feel and love not only your own role —
or some element of it — but also feel and love the audience.
Sounds sentimental, I'm afraid, but there you have it.*
— Sir Laurence Olivier

If you give audiences a chance, they'll do half your acting for you.
— Katharine Hepburn

*Every now and then, when you're on stage, you hear the best sound
a player can hear. It's a sound you can't get in movies or in
television. It is the sound of a wonderful, deep silence that means
you've hit them where they live.*
— Shelley Winters

Just be truthful — and if you can fake that, you've got it made.
— Barbara Stanwyck

*Some of the most intense affairs are between actors and characters.
There's a fire in the human heart and we jump into it with the same
obsession as we have with our lovers.*
— Sigourney Weaver

*The important thing in acting is to be able to laugh and cry.
If I have to cry, I think of my sex life.
If I have to laugh, I think of my sex life.*
— Glenda Jackson

Acting is like making love. It's better if your partner is good, but it's probably possible if your partner isn't.
— Jeremy Irons

I give myself to my parts as to a lover. It's the only way.
— Vanessa Redgrave

Acting is like sex. You should just do it.
— Joanne Woodward

All good actors work the same way.
They just stand there on their own two feet and tell the truth.
— James Woods

Keep it simple. Make a blank face and the music and the
story will fill it in.
— Ingrid Bergman

Come to work on time, know your lines and don't bump into other actors.
— Spencer Tracy

Learn your lines, don't bump into furniture — and in kissing scenes,
keep your mouth closed.
— Ronald Reagan

Talk low, talk slow, and don't talk too much.
— John Wayne

My old drama coach used to say, "Don't just do something, stand there."
— Clint Eastwood

Sometimes, a look is the word.
— Sean Connery

*Listen, I got three expressions: looking left, looking right,
and looking straight ahead.*
— Robert Mitchum

*I think that's our job. To be expressive and daring and go out on a
limb. Everybody should live as big and as authentically as they can.*
— Geena Davis

There is a certain combination of anarchy and discipline
in the way I work.
— Robert De Niro

You spend all your life trying to do something they put people
in asylums for.
— Jane Fonda

Acting is a way of living out one's insanity.
— Isabelle Huppert

Acting is nothing more or less than playing. The idea is to humanize life.
— Jeff Goldblum

The more different the mask you wear, the more of yourself you're going to allow through the mask. The mask is the trick that allows you to be more who you are.
— Kevin Kline

A lot of what acting is is paying attention.
— Robert Redford

*The art of acting is not to act. Once you show them more,
what you show them, in fact, is bad acting.*
— Anthony Hopkins

The art of acting consists of keeping people from coughing.
— Sir Ralph Richardson

As a person, I'm not very interesting. As an actor, I hope I'm riveting.
— Willem Dafoe

A lot of us have a lot of hatred and pain in us —
all the things that make good actors.
— Eddie Murphy

To make it, you have to do one thing that no human really wants to
do: You've got to expose yourself. You can't be afraid.
You can't cover up. That's what separates the men from the boys.
— Jack Lemmon

Life experiences become acting experiences,
which in turn become life experiences.
— Liv Ullman

Acting is experience with something sweet behind it.
— Humphrey Bogart

Without wonder and insight, acting is just a trade.
With it, it becomes creation.
— Bette Davis

To grasp the full significance of life is the actor's duty, to interpret
it is his problem, and to express it his dedication.
— Marlon Brando

Every actor in his heart believes everything bad that's printed about him.
— Orson Welles

If you're obsessed with your destination, you miss 80 percent of the point of acting: the ride there, the people you meet along the way.
— Kevin Costner

Acting is like sustaining a twenty-five-year love affair. There are no new tricks. You just have to keep finding new ways to do it, to keep it fresh.
— Marlon Brando

*First of all, I choose the great {roles}, and if none
of these come, I choose the mediocre ones, and if they don't come,
I choose the ones that pay the rent.*
— Michael Caine

*Of course, I've done my share of idiotic roles, everybody does; Olivier
did idiotic roles. You have to go through that to earn a living. But if
you can make an idiotic role fairly convincing, you've got it made.
When the great one comes along, it's a breeze.*
— Christopher Plummer

The trick is to be the best maid or cook or spear-carrier that you can.
— Agnes Moorehead

If you're going to make rubbish, be the best rubbish in it.
— Richard Burton

Put me in the last fifteen minutes of a picture and I don't care what happened before. I don't even care if I was in the rest of the damn picture — I'll take it in those fifteen minutes.
— Barbara Stanwyck

You never stop learning to act. It isn't that kind of a racket; you never have the thing licked.
— Jimmy Stewart

BOOKS

Adams, Abby, An Uncommon Scold, Simon & Schuster, 1989

Andrews, Robert, ed., The Columbia Dictionary of Quotations,
Columbia University Press, 1993

Auguarde, Tony, ed., The Oxford Dictionary of Modern Quotations,
Oxford University Press, 1991

Blackwell, Earl, Earl Blackwell's Entertainment Celebrity Register,
Visible Ink Press, 1991

Bolander, Donald O., ed., The Instant Quotation Dictionary, Career Publishing, 1987

Boone, Louis E., Quotable Business, Random House, 1992

Bresson, Robert, Notes on the Cinematographer, Sun & Moon Press, 1997

Brown, H. Jackson, A Father's Book of Wisdom, Rutledge Hill Press, 1991

Brown, David, Star Billing: TellTale Trivia from Hollywood,
Weidenfeld & Nicolson Ltd, 1986

Bukowski, Charles, Tales of Ordinary Madness, City Lights, 1984

Buñuel, Luis, My Last Sigh, Random House, 1984

Byrne, Robert, ed., 1,911 Best Things Anybody Ever Said, Ballantine Books, 1988

Cameron, Julia & Byron, Mark, The Artist's Way, J.P. Tarcher Press, 1992

Chandler, Raymond, Raymond Chandler Speaking, Ayer Co., 1977

Columbo, J.R., ed., Columbo's Hollywood, Jonathan-James Books, 1979

RESOURCES

Cosby, Bill, Time Flies, Bantam Books, 1988

Didion, Joan, Slouching Towards Bethlehem, Guilford, 1992

Donadio, S., et al., ed., The NY Public Library Book of 20th Century American Quotations, Warner Books, 1992

Froug, William, The Screenwriter Looks at the Screenwriter, Silman-James Press, 1972

Gordon, Ruth, My Side, Harper Collins, 1976

Halliwell, Leslie, ed., Halliwell's Filmgoer's Book of Quotes, Granada Publishing, 1978

Herman, Gary, ed., The Book of Hollywood Quotes, Omnibus Press, 1979

Jones, James Earl, Voices and Silences, Touchstone Books, 1994

Klein, Allen, ed., Quotations to Cheer You Up When the World Is Getting You Down, Sterling, 1991

Lambray, Maureen, The American Film Directors, Collier Books, 1976

Levine, Michael, ed., Take It From Me, Perigee Books, 1996

Maggio, Rosalie, ed., The Beacon Book of Quotations by Women, Beacon Press 1992

Maisel, Eric, Affirmations for Artists, G.P. Putnam's Sons, 1996

Malloy, Merrit & Sorensen, Shauna, The Quotable Quote Book, Citadel Press, 1990

Peter, Dr. Laurence J., ed., Peter's Quotations: Ideas for Our Time, Bantam Books, 1987

Rodley, Chris, ed., Cronenberg on Cronenberg, Faber & Faber, 1994

Rowes, Barbara, ed., The Book of Quotes, E.P. Dutton, 1979

Safire, William & Safir, Leonard, Good Advice on Writing, Simon & Schuster, 1992

Safire, William & Safir, Leonard, Words of Wisdom: More Good Advice, Simon & Schuster, 1989

Shaughnessy, Susan, Walking On Alligators, Harper, 1993

Shipman, David, Brando, Doubleday, 1975

Shipman, David, ed., Movie Talk, St. Martin's Press, 1991

Smith, Ronald L., ed., The Comedy Quote Dictionary, Doubleday, 1992

Stephens, Autumn, ed., Wild Words from Wild Women, Conari Press, 1996

The Quotable Woman, Running Press, 1991

Warner, Carolyn, ed., The Last Word: A Treasury of Women's Quotes, Prentice-Hall, 1992

Weintraub, Joseph, The Wit & Wisdom of Mae West, Perigee Books, 1981

MAGAZINES & NEWSPAPERS

7 Days

Boston Globe, The

Boston Phoenix, The

Calgary Herald, The

Christian Science Monitor, The

Dallas Times Herald, The

Entertainment Today

Esquire

Extra

Film Monthly

Film Yearbook

Films Illustrated

Films & Filming

KinoRevue

Knave

Life

London Daily Mail, The

London Daily Telegraph, The

London Evening Standard, The

London Independent,

London Observer, The

London Sunday Express, The

London Sunday Times, The

Movieline

New York Times, The

News Summaries

Newsweek

Parade

People

Playboy

Premiere

Ritz, The

Rolling Stone

San Francisco Focus

Screen International

Time

Variety

WGA Journal, The

You: Mail on Sunday Magazine

WEB SITES

The Biz, http://www.bizmag.com
Creative Quotations, http://www.bemorecreative.com/
FilmPlex, http://www.gigaplex.com/film/index.htm
Flicks, http://whyy.org/flicks/
Good Quotes by Famous People, http://www.cs.virginia.edu/~robins/
Michael Moncur's Quotation Server, http://www.starlingtech.com/quotes/
Mr. Showbiz, http://www.mrshowbiz.com
Rough Cut, http://www.roughcut.com/

SOFTWARE

Aapex-Webster's Quotebase, Keith Mohler, Aapex Software, 1993-94
The Columbia Dictionary of Quotations, Bookshelf '94, Microsoft
Corporation, 1994

OTHER BOOKS BY
MICHAEL WIESE PRODUCTIONS

Producer To Producer - 2nd Edition
Surviving Production
The Director's Journey
Fade In - 2nd Edition
The Writer's Journey
Film Directing: Shot By Shot
Film Directing: Cinematic Motion
Film & Video Budgets - 2nd Edition
Film & Video On The Internet
Directing Actors
Persistence Of Vision
Film & Video Financing
The Independent Film & Videomakers Guide
The Search For Reality

To order any of these books and obtain a free catalog
call   1-800-833-5738

Michael Wiese Productions
11288 Ventura Blvd., Suite 821
Studio City, CA 91604

www.mwp.com